JOURNEY LOST TEMPLE

Susannah Leigh

Illustrated by
John Blackman

Front cover illustration by Phillip Burrows
Designed by Kim Blundell
Additional design and artwork by Christopher Gillingwater
Edited by Karen Dolby Series editor: Gaby Waters

Contents

About this Book

Journey to the Lost Temple is an exciting adventure story that takes you on a dangerous jungle trek in search of a fabulous lost temple.

Throughout the book, there are lots of tricky puzzles and perplexing problems which you must solve in order to understand the next part of the story.

Look at the pictures carefully and watch out for vital clues. Sometimes you will need to flick back through the book to help you find an answer. There are extra clues on page 43 and you can check the answers on pages 44 to 48.

Jack's and Em's adventure begins with a letter from their friend, Wanda .

Wanda

Veri Hotee
June 11 th

Dear Jack and Em,
Weather is hot, wish you were here - I need your help. Half of a priceless mask has been stolen from the city museum. Prime suspects are the Bruza Brothers, notorious art thieves. Now the mask's other half, hidden in the legendary lost temple, is in danger. It must be saved. The peace of Wat-A-Skor-Cha depends on it. Let me explain about the legend...

Jack   Em

Wanda Pharr is a famous explorer, working in the hot and hilly country of Wat-A-Skor-Cha. Turn the page to continue her letter.

The Legend of the Lost Temple

The story goes something like this...

Long ago, deep in the jungle of Wat-A-Skor-Cha, an ancient and wonderful temple was discovered. No one knew who had built it or why it was there. Inside was a room full of magnificent masks. One of them was made of a shimmery golden metal which glowed eerily in the darkness.. Its left eye was a priceless emerald and its right a perfect ruby...

Until then, the people of Wat-A-Skor-Cha had lived peacefully for hundreds of years. But the moment they saw the mask, a strange feeling came over each of them. They could not tear their eyes from its glow and each person's only wish was to possess the mask. They began arguing and a fierce struggle broke out. In the confusion there was an ear-splitting crack and the mask broke into two pieces.

At once there was silence. The people looked in terror at the two halves. The mask's glow had gone. Its spell was broken and the people no longer wanted to fight. But they knew if the mask were put together again its mysterious power would return and they were afraid.

So they decided to bring one half of the mask back to the town where it was kept in the museum. The right half with the ruby eye was left in the temple. This way its strange power would be controlled. Since that time the two halves have remained safely apart. The temple lies deep in the middle of the jungle but the way there has long been forgotten and the jungle is dangerous and deadly. Many have tried to find it, but none have returned...

Interesting story eh? I suspect the Bruza Brothers stole the mask from the museum and are now on their way to the temple to steal the ruby half of the mask as well. I can think of only one way to beat them. I must find the temple and retrieve its half mask before they do...Your puzzle-solving minds would be a great help.

Yours in desperation - Wanda xxx

4

J ack folded the letter. They had taken up Wanda's challenge and arrived in Wat-A-Skor-Cha. Their heads were buzzing with questions. Most important of all, Em wanted to find out more about the Bruza Brothers. All she knew was that they were ruthless crooks – cigar-smoking Bill Bruza and his slimy brother, Brian.

Now they had to meet Wanda. Below them was the valley of Veri-Hotee where she lived. Jack turned the envelope over to read the return address. Looking down at the huts again, he saw it was easy to work it out.

Which is Wanda's house?

FROM: Wanda Pharr
The Brown Hut
Tree View
Lakeside

Veri Hotee
W - A - S

AIRMAIL

AIRMAIL

5

Wanda Explains

Jack and Em peered through the door of Wanda's little house.

"Jack, Em!" she cried. "Come in. I'll tell you what's been going on."

"The night after the mask was stolen from the museum, an ancient map, showing the route back from the lost temple to Veri-Hotee, was taken from my hut," she explained. "I'm sure it was the Bruza's work again."

"The Bruzas haven't been seen since the break in," she continued. "They must be on their way to the temple . . . and the other half of the mask. When the mask is completed, they will hold its strange power and who knows what they will do with it then."

"Sounds a bit far-fetched to me," Jack said.

"I don't know if the legend is true," Wanda replied. "But the complete mask is priceless . . . a work of art. It musn't fall into the hands of the crooked Bruzas."

"So we MUST reach the temple before them," gasped Em. "But how do we get there without the map?"

"Well," began Wanda, sheepishly. "I believe there IS a copy of the map in the safe belonging to my predecessor, the esteemed travel writer, Ima Homesic. But the safe hasn't been opened for so long, I can't remember the combination."

"There must be a way into it," said Jack, peering at the dial.

"I THINK it's a six number sequence. It starts with a one," said Wanda, thinking hard. "And there's a four in there somewhere . . ."

"Then it's easy to work out," said Em.

What is the sequence that opens the safe?

The Mysterious Map

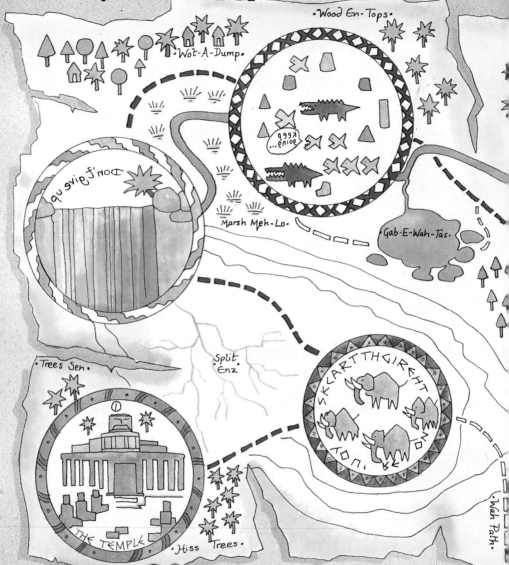

The dial clicked and the safe door swung open. Wanda lifted out a roll of yellowing parchment and spread it carefully on the table. Jack and Em stared at the ancient document.

There were strange pictures in circles joined by dotted lines.

"The red lines must show the route back from the temple," Wanda said.

"I think the pictures are landmarks," she continued. "If each is found in the right order, they should lead to the temple."

"Where do we begin?" asked Em.

Jack looked at the circles and noticed some strange writing.

"I know what to do!" he said.

Do you?

The Journey Begins

Early next morning, Wanda finally finished stuffing her explorer's back pack with all the handy equipment vital for their dangerous journey.

At last they set off. They climbed up into the wooded hills above the valley, away from the village, safety and civilization in search of the Greenus Lobie.

Further on, they came to a clearing in the middle of the jungle. Clusters of colourful flowers were dotted around.

"This must be it," said Wanda.

"But which flower is the right one?" asked Em.

"That's easy," Jack replied, as he pulled a dog-eared book on jungle plants from his back pack.

All around were tropical trees and bushes. There was no path and they had to fight their way through sharp bamboo and prickly shrubbery.

They were soon puffing and panting their way up a steep hill. The ground was stony and rocks crumbled and slipped beneath their feet.

Wat-A-Skor-Cha Flora

LOBUS BLUENESS
Long stemmed. Flowers may be purple, red or yellow. Tree loving.

LOBUS STINKUS
Indented leaves. Deadly poisonous. Flowers red from October to January and purple from February to September.

LOBUS FLUTTERBY
Purple or red flowers. Attracts butterflies.

GREENUS LOBIE
Indented leaves. Flowers purple October to December and red January to September. Harmless.

CREEPING LOBIE
Non-flowering climber. Grows up tree trunks.

LOBIE FLYTRAP
Red or yellow flowers. Eats insects. Indented leaves.

LOBUS SHADUS
Light blue flower. Tree and shade loving.

He turned to the right page and puzzled over the descriptions. Em and Wanda examined the flowers. It wasn't going to be so easy after all. Several of the flowers looked exactly the same.

Jack read his book carefully and looked very hard at the plants. Soon he was able to work it out.

Which is the Greenus Lobie?

Which Way?

Jack knelt down and put the compass directly above the clump of Greenus Lobie and took a bearing. Due east was a path through the forest.

"What's the next landmark?" asked Wanda, as they set off along the narrow path which twisted and turned through the thick jungle.

"Some strange stone heads," said Em, looking at the map.

Straight ahead through the trees, the three explorers caught sight of a small village with a few round huts.

As they drew nearer, several people came out to meet them. Em asked them for directions.

The trio listened in dismay to the different directions. Which was the right route? Wanda couldn't work it out.

"There's only one thing for it." she sighed. "We'll take the first route. If that fails, we'll do the rest in order."

Jack and Em reluctantly agreed with her. They started off along the jungle path following the first set of instructions.

Where does the first route take them?
What about the other routes?

Message in the Stones

Five minutes and one deadly-looking snake pit later, Jack and Em began to wish that Wanda hadn't chosen the first route. But soon after, they were amazed and surprised to find they were where they wanted to be – at the strange stone heads.

"The power of the mask must be on our side," Wanda grinned.

The giant, carved heads stood in a large circle and were all different shapes. On the ground were broken bits of rock and stone. Em was puzzled. What was the secret of the heads? They certainly looked very sinister. Were they meant to search for an instruction or message? Perhaps the ancient map itself held the answer.

She sat down on a rock, took the map from her back pack and unrolled it. She read it carefully, hoping for inspiration. But without knowing what to look for, it wasn't easy. Suddenly it came to her in a flash, and looking at all the stones again, she quickly saw where to go next.

What has Em noticed?

Swamped!

The arrow directed the three explorers west. The shrieks and cackles of tropical birds and the calls of strange jungle animals echoed around them as they journeyed slowly along deep gulleys filled with strange shrubs and odd creatures. Suddenly they stopped. Directly in front of them was a large mangrove swamp.

"We'll never get across this," Jack groaned. "And we can't go round, the jungle's too thick."

"We could wade across," suggested Em, hopefully.

"No. It's too dangerous," Wanda replied. "That slime looks deep."

She pulled a long stick from the bank and plunged it into the marsh. It sank slowly, disappearing with a loud gurgle.

Jack shuddered as he thought of all the nasty things that might be lurking in the slime. He looked at the jungle surrounding the swamp and saw overhanging branches and thick creepers. A plan formed in his mind and he saw how to cross.

What is Jack's plan?

The Missing Clue

The swamp came to a shallow, sticky end. The trio struggled on ankle-deep in the murky water. Em led the way, trying to keep a sure footing as she followed the submerged path to firm ground. Flies buzzed noisily around Wanda's head as she ducked their angry attack. Meanwhile Jack felt a strange sensation on his arm. He looked down and saw leeches greedily slurping at his skin.

Deeper in the jungle, long vines hung down from the trees and swung in their faces, and scratchy thorn bushes grew close to the ground. Luckily, Wanda had remembered her handy jungle walking stick and they could cut their way through.

Jack began to feel very miserable. Sweat slowly trickled down his back and he wondered if they were heading in the right direction. It was getting hotter and hotter.

They stuck closely behind Wanda and when she stopped suddenly, Em and Jack tumbled over. As they picked themselves up from the ground, they saw a tall, stone plinth among the trees.

"The statue!" gasped Jack.

"Not any more," groaned Wanda, and she was right – the base was empty and the statue had gone.

"It could have been missing for centuries," Jack pointed out.

But Em was not so sure. Looking closely at the base of the statue, she knew it had been stolen very recently. And what's more, she could name the thieves.

What has Em spotted?
Who are the thieves?

All Tied Up

Suddenly Em felt a hand on her shoulder. She spun round quickly to find herself face to face with a large, round-faced man. He wore a big hat and from his thin mouth dangled a fat cigar. He was very scary.

"Gotcha!" snarled Bill Bruza. "But unfortunately for you, this is the last puzzle you'll be solving for a very long time."

"Maybe forever," giggled his slimy brother, Brian.

Jack gulped. He had heard so much about the evil pair, but he'd never imagined they would look so villainous. He shivered as the gruesome twosome circled slowly around them.

Brian Bruza tied the trio's hands and Bill pushed them roughly on into the dark jungle. The captives stumbled and tripped over the bumpy ground until they came to a group of tall trees.

"Stop here, this is far enough," growled Bill as he tied Wanda, Jack and Em to three sturdy trees. "This is where your journey ends."

"If the wild animals don't eat you first, you'll starve," Brian cackled, following his brother away into the jungle.

The prisoners looked at each other in despair. Was this the end? They shivered in spite of the heat as the same thought crossed their minds. Were they to be lion food that night? They tried to struggle free, but it was useless. Their hands seemed to be firmly tied.

How can they escape?

Crossing the Crocodile Creek

Jack tugged at his ropes – a quick release knot! He wriggled his hands free.

"Those Bruzas need a lesson in knot tying," he laughed, as he unknotted the cords around Wanda's and Em's wrists.

In the distance they could hear running water and in a flash Wanda remembered the map. It must be the waterfall! They set off at a run in the direction of the noise. Soon they arrived at a grassy bank. Across the river was the waterfall. Stepping stones and logs made a path to the other side of the bank.

"Let's cross here!" said Jack, about to hop onto the first log.

"Watch out!" cried Em. "It's not a log, it's a crocodile!"

Swiftly Jack jumped back. Em was right. And now Jack saw that some of the stones looked like hippos. They even had flies buzzing around them.

"What do we do now?" he asked.

"Follow me," said Wanda. "I think I can see a way across."

Can you find a safe route across the river avoiding the watery creatures?

The Waterfall Surprise

They scrambled onto the rocky shore. The waterfall crashed and cascaded around them and spray from the water splashed their faces.

"What next?" yelled Em, above the roar of the fall.

"This is useless," Jack moaned, sitting down glumly on a rock. "How can this waterfall lead us to the temple?"

"We can't give up now," said Wanda. "We've got to find the temple before the Bruzas. They must be way ahead of us."

"Perhaps we'll be able to see from the top," said Em, beginning to climb the rocks at the side of the fall. Wanda was right behind.

Reluctantly Jack followed them. He was feeling very miserable and hungry, and his boots were full of water. But the climb was easier then it looked. There were handy foot holds in the rock.

Just then Em caught sight of something amazing. This could be what they were looking for.

"Look over there," she yelled.

They inched themselves across to investigate and saw a narrow gap between two boulders. Jack and Wanda could hardly believe their eyes when they peered through the hole and saw a rocky staircase, ending in darkness. Jack felt excited as they slipped between the rocks and crept down the steps.

At the bottom was a dimly-lit chamber. Rocks grew from the roof and floor. But there was nothing else to see. The trail seemed to have run dry. Now it was Em's turn to feel glum.

"It's a dead end," she said.

Jack was leaning against the wall when he gave a shout.

"Look at this!" he yelled and pointed to a small wooden lever sticking out from a stone slab. Eagerly he tugged it.

WHOOSH! There was a rushing sound and the floor gave way. Their stomachs dropped as they fell down and down a rocky chute. CRASH. They landed at the bottom in the gloomy darkness.

25

Cryptic Code

There was silence followed by a soft rustling sound. Jack shivered and Em's skin tingled.

"Its only me," said Wanda cheerfully. "I'm looking for the torches in my back pack."

Em wished she would hurry. It was dark and creepy in the cave. The sound of dripping water came from far away and strange creatures squeaked in the silence. At last Wanda handed her a torch and she clicked it on.

"Come on," Wanda said. "We've got to work out where to go now."

Her voice trailed away as she shone the torch into the inky blackness and gasped at what she found there.

Dead ahead was a rock face. Carved into it was a square frame. It was covered with rows and rows of strange symbols.

"What is it?" whispered Jack, peering at the squiggles.

"It's an old Wat-A-Skor-Cha cypher," Wanda replied. "They were used by the ancient people for very secret messages. There were lots of different ones."

"Amazing!" she continued. "It's the cypher I was studying before we left. I have my notes with me."

She showed Em and Jack her work, but it wasn't complete.

"If we fit the letters to the symbols shown here, the rest of the message might fall into place," said Em thoughtfully.

What do the symbols say?

Jumbled Jigsaw

The cypher said their goal was getting closer, but first they had to find the green crystals. They were just wondering which way to turn when Em spotted a small, narrow passageway at the back of the cave. She squeezed through to investigate.

"In here!" she called, her voice echoing through the hollow cave.

Jack and Wanda speedily followed her. They found themselves in a large, round cavern. Shadows lengthened on the walls and water dripped slowly from the cracked rock. But the cool air was refreshing after the hot, sticky jungle.

"Quick. Over here with the torch," Em called.

She was standing by the far wall of the cavern. From a distance it looked rough and worn. But there was something interesting about it . . .

In the torchlight they saw that it was covered with strange pictures, but there were also gaps in the wall where the bare rock showed through.

At their feet lay pieces of stone with more pictures painted on them. They came from the spaces in the wall where the rock had crumbled away.

"Maybe it's another clue." said Em. "Perhaps we should work out where these pieces fit in."

What does the painting show?

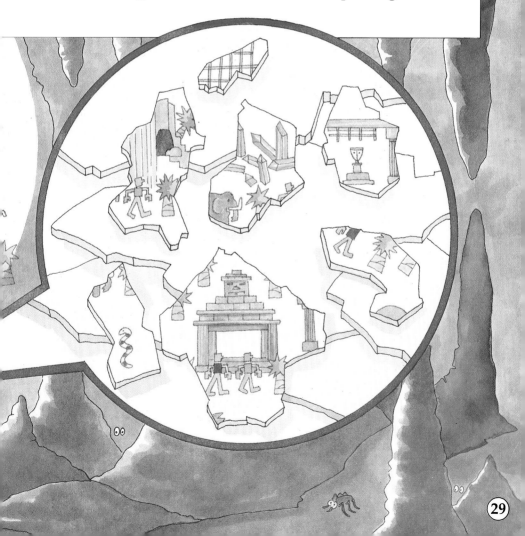

Elephant Walk

It was exciting to see the temple in pictures, but they hadn't learnt anything new. At that moment their attention was distracted by a shining light in the corner of the cave . . . the green crystals! They hurried over and scrabbled through the glowing rocks. But the key wasn't there.

"The Bruzas have beaten us to it!" groaned Em.

"Then we must hurry to catch up with them," Wanda said.

Jack spotted a small gap in the roof above them. Cut into the walls were foot and hand holds.

Breathless, the three scrambled out of the cave, onto a high, rocky plateau. The land around was desert-like, but in the distance the jungle started again. Wanda pulled her binoculars from her back pack and tried to get her bearings.

Suddenly she gasped. Far away was a tiny dot. Hardly daring to believe her eyes, Wanda peered through the lenses. At last . . . the temple! It was just visible through the distant tree tops. They set the compass and began their final trek.

The sun beat down as they crossed the plain. Just when they thought they could go no further, Wanda spotted three hefty elephants. She remembered the map.

"Let's hitch a lift," she said.

She gently tapped one on its front knee. The elephant knelt down and Wanda climbed onto his back.

"It's OK," she said. "I'm an expert at this."

Jack and Em did the same. And at a word from Wanda, the strange procession set off.

Em was surprised to find the ride so uncomfortable, but it was better than walking. Soon they had left the desert and were trekking into jungle again. They climbed down from the elephants and left them at a pool, then walked on through the trees.

Suddenly they stopped. They were at the edge of a high cliff – and far below was the temple. Would they ever reach it? They HAD to find a way down the cliff. Then Wanda had a brainwave.

How can they get down?

The Temple

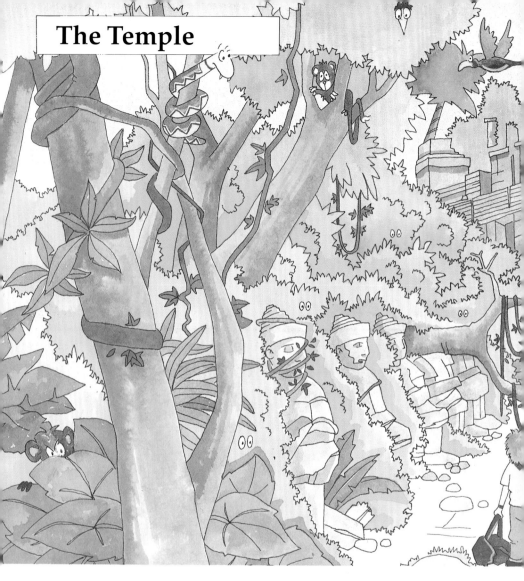

Their pulses raced as they neared their final goal. Suddenly there it was, tall and imposing . . . the lost temple. Ancient stone statues lined the path to the heavy doors and carved faces glared down at them. Creepers had grown over the temple walls, but it was still magnificent. They had arrived.

"But it's no good," said Jack, staring at the temple. "We don't have the key to get in."

Em marched up to the heavy iron doors. She heaved and pushed with all her might, but they wouldn't budge. She peered through the keyhole and saw nothing but blackness.

"We're too late," she wailed. "The Bruzas must have locked the door behind them. Now the whole mask is in their power and it will never belong to Wat-A-Skor-Cha again."

"We can't give up now after all we've been through," said Wanda. "There must be another way in."

But they found no other door. Their brains whirred. What was their next move? Em looked in frustration at the temple again. It was then that she remembered something important. If her hunch was right there was another way inside.

How can they get into the temple?

Monkey Business

Em climbed the statue and with a great tug, turned the head around. There was a grating sound and a small panel in the side of the temple slid open. Cautiously they stepped through into the dark. To his horror, Jack saw hundreds of pairs of eyes staring back at him.

"Someone else is here," gasped Wanda. "Switch on the torch."

WHOOSH. A small, brown, furry creature swung past Em's ear. The room was full of chattering monkeys, swinging from creepers and hanging from the walls.

They scanned the room and quickly realized the mask wasn't there. They walked on into a cold, narrow corridor which curved round to the right.

Statues lined the walls. The passage ended and they turned right into a wider corridor, left past a snake mosaic and then first right.

Next left was a dead end, but it led them to a plan of the temple. In the centre was a mask. This HAD to be the mask room they were looking for.

Jack tried to remember their route so far.

Where are they now? How can they get to the mask room?

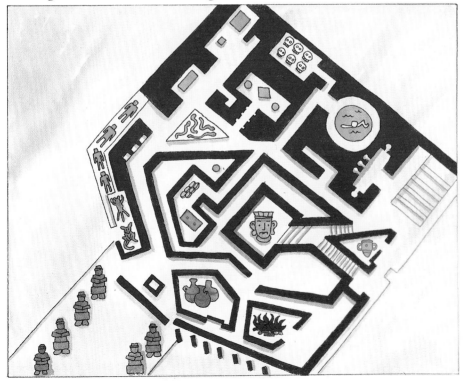

The Bruzas Return

Minutes later they reached the room at the centre of the temple. It was filled with masks. Some were whole, but most were broken.

But there was no time to look for the temple's ruby-eyed half mask. At that moment they heard footsteps and familiar voices behind them.

It was the Bruza Brothers. Bill snarled gruffly at slimy Brian, who giggled. Then they stared menacingly at the trio who were cornered again.

Bill lunged for Jack but he dived through Bill's legs. Wanda tripped Brian who went flying. Then Em spotted something in Bill's bag and a desperate plan formed in her head. It was their only chance . . .

She grabbed a creeper and with a yell, swung from it, aiming for Bill's bag. A direct hit! Before bewildered Bill knew what was happening, the emerald-eyed mask had catapulted from his bag.

It fell through the air. With a sickening thud it landed beside Jack who tried not to worry about the way the mask was being thrown about. Bungling Brian dived to grab it, but Jack got there first.

Jack threw the mask to Wanda just as Brian reached him. Now it was Wanda's turn to dodge the slimy pair. Falling over themselves in their desperate attempts to grab the mask, the Bruzas stumbled towards Wanda.

Swiftly she dodged the crooks and running around behind them, quickly passed the mask to Em, who was hiding behind a large statue. The Bruzas were dizzy. They just weren't quick enough to outwit the trio.

Over here, I've got a plan!

But Jack, Em and Wanda were tiring. They had to escape with the mask, but how? As they dodged the Bruzas' evil clutches, Jack had a feeling he had seen this room somewhere before.

He thought over what he had learned about the temple so far. Then he realized the room held the secret to trapping the Bruzas. If he could only find the lever... He grabbed the mask and ran.

He reached the corner of the room, both Bruzas in hot pursuit. Jack spun round to dodge them. The brothers collided and Jack darted across to the wall.

What is Jack's plan?

The Missing Mask

Jack speedily yanked a rusty handle and there was a loud, whirring sound. Before the Bruzas had time to pick themselves up, a heavy wooden grid crashed down across a corner of the room. The Bruzas were trapped behind it.

"Good work," grinned Wanda. "We'll have to trek to the nearest village for help with the crooks."

Jack held the half mask that the Bruzas had stolen from the museum and looked at it closely for the first time. Its emerald eye winked back at him.

"We must find its other half," Em said. "Don't forget the cypher."

The room was full of relics. There were statues, idols and hundreds of broken masks. Finding the right half seemed impossible. Then, out of the corner of her eye, Wanda saw something shining. If the old legend about the mask was right, she had found its other half, left in the temple for centuries.

Where is the temple's half mask?

The Temple Remains

Carefully, Wanda held both halves of the mask in her hands. Jack and Em watched with bated breath as Wanda hesitated, wondering whether she should put it back together.

All of a sudden there was a bright flash and the mask jumped out of Wanda's hands. As if by magic, it was whole again. The ground shook and a shower of rocks fell from the ceiling.

"Lets get out of here!" cried Em. "The roof's caving in."

But a frightened shout made her turn around quickly. The Bruzas were still trapped. Quickly Jack pushed the lever. The grill slid up and the Bruzas raced away. They sped out of the temple with petrified yells.

The temple was collapsing fast. Stone slabs crashed down around them. Em and Wanda dashed to the door and on through the maze of corridors to the temple's exit. Jack was right behind, but stopped to look back at the mask. It was shaking and glowing. Jack shuddered and sprinted out just before the roof gave way.

He reached the safety of the jungle just in time. There was a final loud crack as the temple disappeared in a cloud of dust. Coughing and spluttering, Wanda, Em and Jack stared speechless at the ruins.

"The mask was more powerful than we thought," gasped Em finally. "But at least no one can take it now. It's vanished for ever."

Or has it?

41

What Happened Next . . .

Dear Jack and Em,
Hope you enjoyed the rest of your holiday and that you got back safely. Just a quick note to say thank you so much for your help. I couldn't have done it without you! I thought you might be interested in the enclosed press cuttings. Things certainly haven't been quiet around here since you left. Anyway, keep in touch, and let's meet again soon, OK? I promise a relaxing holiday next time.

love, Wanda
xxx

Daily Skorcha - July 20th

FETE SUCCESS
The annual Wat-A-Skor-Cha orphanage garden fete on Saturday was a grand success, raising a lot of money for charity. In particular, the tombola was a great favourite with the excited crowds. The fete was ceremoniously opened by Mr Bill Bruza, the orphanage's newly appointed head governor.

SHADY DEALS
His appointment came as some surprise to those who know of his former activities in the world of petty theft and shady deals. However his recent, and very generous, foray into the world of children's charities has shown his sincerity to reform.

SUPERNATURAL
We asked Bill why he had given all his money to charity, and where his brother and ex-partner in crime, Brian was. Mr Bruza's reply was very vague. He hinted at strange supernatural experiences and some children who'd saved his life. "My brother Brian?" Bill concluded. "He's taken a very long holiday in the Caribbean."

'Wat-A-Skor-Cha World' July 22nd

TEMPLE UPDATE
Many explorers have tried – and failed – to follow the trail to the lost temple, first blazed by local girl, explorer Wanda Pharr, and her two young assistants Jack and Em. Wanda, who made her intrepid journey last month heroically prevented the fabulous mask of the temple from falling into the hands of two villainous thieves.

MYSTERIOUS
After a reported earthquake destroyed the temple, the mask disappeared under the ruins. However, it was never clear if the mask really had been lost for ever.

CHANCE DISCOVERY
Further light was shed on this question recently when a group of botanists, led by the distinguished scientist, Teresa Green, stumbled upon the ruined temple. Ms Green and her party had lost their way in the jungle while searching for the rare Orchid Narcotica plant, when they made their chance discovery of the Lost Temple.

Teresa Green

SWALLOWED UP
"We spotted the famous mask glinting among the rubble," Ms Green told us exclusively. "One of my team reached out to grab it. At the same moment the earth shook and began to crack. There was a roar of thunder, although it was a clear day. Then sparks flew – it was really spooky. We jumped back just in time. The ground in front of us opened up and swallowed the temple, mask and all. With a final shudder it closed again. There was nothing left at all of the Lost Temple."

THE TRUTH? ...d's comment.
There is no doubt that the story of the lost temple and its fabulous mask is a strange one. Could there be some truth in the old legend about the mask's strange powers after all? Surely not, although perhaps you should make up your own minds . . .

from 'The Skorch' July 26th

Brian Bruza

BRIAN BRUZA'S BOPPER
Crazy about dancing? Crazy about having a good time? Just plain crazy? Nip over to the island of Ripee-Offee in the Caribbean and experience the magic and lights of a dynamite Disco – **BRIAN BRUZA'S BOPPER**. Truly a night to remember.
★First night party **MASKED BALL!**★

Clues

Answers

Pages 4-5

Wanda's address describes the location of her house.

This is Wanda's house ➤

Pages 6-7

The combination that opens the safe is 1,4,7,10,13,16. The numbers form a sequence, with the numbers increasing by three each time.

Pages 8-9

Jack has realized the circled landmarks have clues written around them. The flower picture is marked number 7. The temple is marked number 1. This suggests that the trail runs backwards from the temple to the village. There are only seven circled landmarks, so the flower picture is the first clue on the trail from Veri-Hotee. The writing around it is in a continuous line. With spacing added it says: W(est) from Veri Hotee to the valley of flowers. Then E(ast) from the Greenus Lobie flower.

The words around the stone heads are written backwards. They say: Use your eyes.

The writing around the elephants is also backwards. It says: You're on the right trail.

The messages on the crocodile and waterfall pictures are in mirror writing. They say: Keep going, and: Don't give up.

Pages 10-11

There is only one plant that fits the description of the Greenus Lobie in the book. As the month is June (see Wanda's letter on page 3), the book tells you the Greenus Lobie's petals are red.

The Greenus Lobie is ringed in black.

Pages 12-13

In fact, all the routes lead to the stones, they just follow different paths. Each is marked in the picture.

KEY:

Route A ————

Route B ————

Route C ————

Pages 14-15

Em has noticed a stone arrow. It has the same markings as the border around the stone head picture on the map.

Here is the arrow ————

Pages 16-17

This is Jack's plan:

1) Using the branches, they climb up this tree.

6) They walk along this branch to the shore.

2) They inch along this branch and drop down to this small island.

5) They can then use this stepping stone to reach the tree trunk.

3) They break off this forked stick and use it to hook the creeper.

4) Next they swing across to this island.

Pages 18-19

Em has spotted three things:

1. Vines which cover the plinth have not yet grown over the spot where the statue stood, suggesting it has been stolen recently.
2. There are fresh footprints leading up to and away from the plinth that don't match the pattern of Jack's,

Em's and Wanda's shoes. (You can see the underside of their shoes on page 18.) This suggests someone has been here just before them.
3. There is a smouldering cigar in the bushes. Em knows that Bill Bruza smokes a cigar, and so she concludes that the Bruzas are the thieves.

Pages 20-21

Jack's hands have only been tied with a quick release knot. If he pulls the end of the rope, the knot will come undone easily. The ropes around Wanda's and Em's hands are more securely tied.

Pages 22-23

The safe route across the river is marked in black.

Pages 26-27

To decode the cypher, first change all the symbols marked in Wanda's notebook to their corresponding letter, e.g. ⋈ = A and / = I etc. When you have done this, you should be able to work out the rest of the letters to make up the words.

Here is the message decoded, with punctuation added:

The temple gates are locked you will see. But under green crystals in this cave is the key.
If all else fails and the key you cannot find, Turn the head that looks behind.
But a warning to all who enter that place, If you have in your hands the emerald-eyed face,
It must be rejoined with its ruby-eyed mate –
This action alone seals the temple's fate.

Pages 28-29

This is what the picture looks like when complete. It shows the ancient people journeying back from the temple.

Pages 30-31

Wanda has a rope in her back pack (see page 10). If they tie it to the sturdy rock at the top of the cliff, they can use it to scramble down.

Pages 32-33

Em spots that this statue's head is facing the wrong way.
She remembers the line from the cryptic message in the cave (pages 26 to 27). "If all else fails . . . turn the head that looks behind." She realizes this must be the head it is referring to.

Pages 34-35

The route they have just taken is marked in black. The way to the mask room is marked in green.

They started here

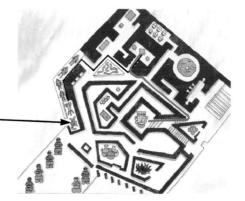

Pages 36-37

Jack has seen the room before in the wall painting on pages 28 to 29. From this he knows that when the lever on the wall is pulled, a grill falls down, cutting off a corner of the room to protect the mask. He realizes that if he lures the Bruzas to this corner of the room, he can trap them behind the grill.

Pages 38-39

Here is the mask's other half.

The legend says that the mask's left half has an emerald eye, and its right a ruby eye. Jack is holding the emerald half. This means they have to look for the mask's right half with the ruby eye.

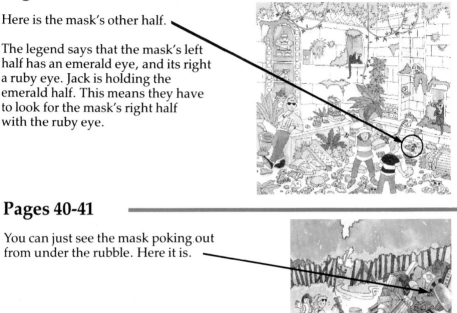

Pages 40-41

You can just see the mask poking out from under the rubble. Here it is.

This edition first published in 2007 by Usborne Publishing Ltd., Usborne House, 83-85 Saffron Hill, London EC1N 8RT, England. www.usborne.com Copyright © 2007, 2001, 1994, 1993 Usborne Publishing Ltd.